May I Quote You,
General Forrest?

MAY I QUOTE YOU, GENERAL FORREST?

Observations and Utterances of the South's Great Generals

Randall Bedwell

CUMBERLAND HOUSE

PUBLISHING INC.

Copyright ©1997 by Randall Bedwell.
Published by Cumberland House Publishing, Inc., 431 Harding Industrial
Drive, Nashville, Tennessee 37211.

May I Quote You. . . ?® is a Registered Trademark of Guild Bindery
Press, Inc.

Some quotes have been edited for clarity and brevity.

Managing Editor: Carol Boker
Associate Editor: Hollis Dodge
Contributing Editors: Palmer Jones, Jim Vaden, Debbie Petite
Historical Advisors: Edward F. Williams III, Jim Fox

Typography: The BookSetters Co.
Text design: The BookSetters Co.
Cover design: Patterson Graham Design Group.

Library of Congress Cataloging-in-Publication Data

May I quote you, General Forrest? : observations and utterances of the
    South's great generals / [compiled by] Randall Bedwell.
        p.   cm.   —(May I quote you, General? series)
    ISBN 1-888952-35-0 (pbk. : alk. paper)
    1. Forrest, Nathan Bedford, 1821-1877—Quotations. 2. United States—
History—Civil War, 1861-1865—Quotations, maxims, etc. 3. Quotations
American.   I. Bedwell, Randall J. II. Series.
E467.1.F72M45 1997
973.73092—dc21   96-51928
                                                                         CIP

Printed in the United States of America
2 3 4 5 6 7 8—01 00 99 98 97

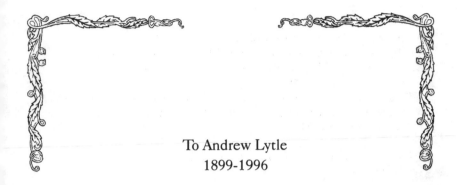

To Andrew Lytle
1899-1996

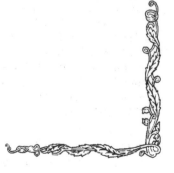

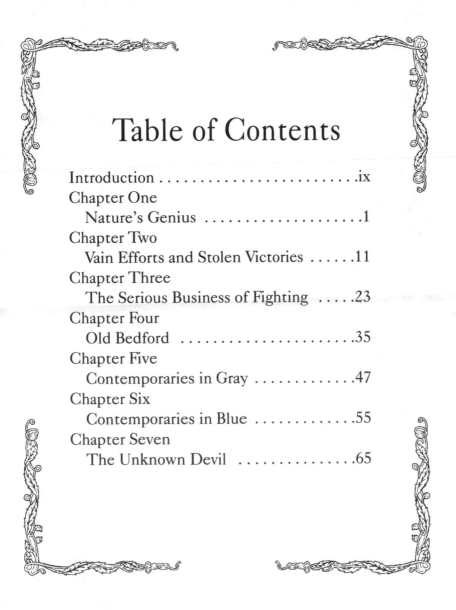

Table of Contents

Introduction

By 1863, Nathan Bedford Forrest had master-minded several successful raids and stunningly captured forces numerically superior to his own—all without the so-called benefits of a formal military education. Despite these successes, the turning point in Forrest's career as a soldier did not come until after the Battle of Chickamauga. His brilliant direction of the cavalry on the right flank that fateful September day (coupled with an irreparable breach with his commanding officer, General Braxton Bragg) garnered him an independent command in North Mississippi and West Tennessee, a district forever after known as "Forrest's Territory." President Jefferson Davis himself authorized Forrest's new duties after a face-to-face interview with the rebel general in Montgomery.

Beset by rapidly consolidating Federal forces and fully aware of unfavorable numerical and logistical realities, Forrest realized his job was not to occupy territory but to deny it to the enemy. To this end, he developed a method of waging war based on speed and concentration of firepower that allowed his troops to defeat larger, conventional forces. Nowhere were the fruits of his genius more evident than at Brice's Crossroads, called by some "the perfect battle."

Forrest's military achievements are the more remarkable when one considers that his command was raised almost entirely within enemy lines. Faced with the passive hostility of the Southern people and their aid—both overt and covert—to Forrest, the Federals regarded every inhabitant of the territory as a potential enemy. General William T. Sherman wrote: "It is none of our business to protect a people that has sent all its youth, and arms, and horses, all that is of any account to war against us. Forrest may cavort around that country as much as he pleases. Every conscript they now catch will cost a good man to watch."

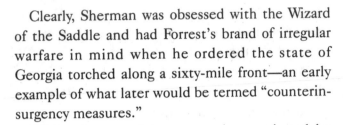

Clearly, Sherman was obsessed with the Wizard of the Saddle and had Forrest's brand of irregular warfare in mind when he ordered the state of Georgia torched along a sixty-mile front—an early example of what later would be termed "counterinsurgency measures."

While the wartime reputations enjoyed by Confederate commanders like Beauregard and Hood have been diminished by successive generations of historians dating back to their own era, Forrest has been acclaimed a wonder of nature. If anything, his legend continues to grow, a living vindication of his unerring instinct for finding a way to win. At Fort Donelson, for instance, he avoided a needless surrender while the professionals were all too ready to stack their arms. Ulysses S. Grant, who subjugated Fort Donelson and in the process made his first giant stride toward the White House, wrote in his memoirs, "Anything that could have prolonged the war a year beyond the time that it did finally close would probably have exhausted the North to such an extent that they might then have abandoned the contest and agreed to a separation." Very likely, Forrest's tactics demonstrated a way to win a kind of protracted war the North most feared.

As Confederate arms collapsed on all fronts, Forrest, whose name was synonymous with victory, refused the temptation of escape to Mexico to avoid the threat of arrest as a war criminal for his controversial actions at Fort Pillow. Instead, he remained with his troops and did that which galled him most; he surrendered. From that moment on, he advocated peace. Apart from a short-lived resort to clandestine activities during the harshest days of military occupation, Forrest's public statements and actions beginning with his farewell address to his soldiers unequivocally favored reconciliation and the rule of law.

Randall Bedwell
Cordova, Tennessee
July 1996

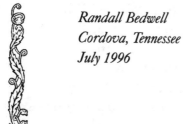

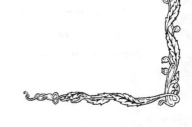

In war men are nothing; a man is every-thing.

—*Napoleon Bonaparte*

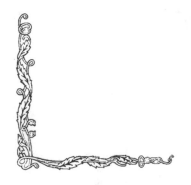
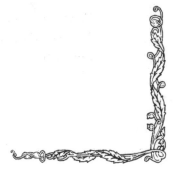

Nathan Bedford Forrest

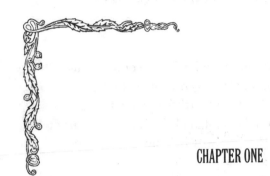

CHAPTER ONE

Nature's Genius

Responding to a question posed by his nephew after the war, General Joseph E. Johnston, Forrest's erstwhile superior officer in the Army of Tennessee, reflected on the career of the Confederacy's most effective soldier: "Forrest, who, had he the advantages of a thoroughly military education and training," Johnston speculated, "would have been the great central figure of the Civil War." High praise, indeed. Yet, the assertion may not be altogether sound. After all, did West Point teach its graduates to throw unprotected artillery forward in hot pursuit of the enemy? No, but Forrest did just that, and the effect was devastating. Would a West Point graduate be trained to rely on his own unsurpassed guile to win battles, sometimes without even firing a shot? Doubtful, but Forrest had faith in his own shrewdness, and the lives of his men were preserved to fight another day.

In the unique case of Nathan Bedford Forrest, a man endowed with a superior, steady intellect bolstered by lightning-quick frontier cunning, a formal military education might well have stifled his natural genius for battlefield improvisation. At the beginning of the Civil War—the threshold of warfare's modern era—no one yet realized that within months textbook military science would be practically obsolete. Hence, Forrest's lack of formal military training left him unencumbered by the outmoded ideas in the cavalry manual, in particular the rigidly defined role of the cavalry branch itself. Horses provided rapid transport but were of little use in a fight except at close quarters with sabers drawn—a worst-case scenario in Forrest's estimation. Once the battleground was chosen, Forrest ordered his hussars to dismount, take cover, and fight like infantry, concentrating their fire. John Allen Wyeth, author of Forrest's first complete biography, wrote, "It may justly be claimed that he established this important feature of warfare [use of mounted infantry] as a part of military science."

I ain't no graduate of West Point and never rubbed my back up against any college.

—*Nathan Bedford Forrest, clarifying his credentials*
for Union Captain Lewis Hosea, 1865

Be careful always to move by interior lines and strike the fragments of your enemy's forces with the masses of your own.

—*P. G. T. Beauregard to Braxton Bragg*

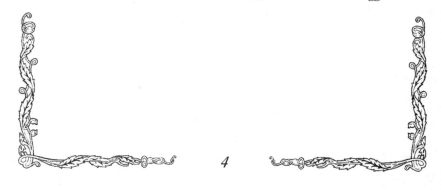

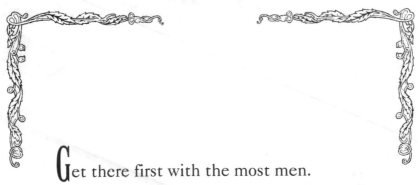

Get there first with the most men.

—Nathan Bedford Forrest expressing Beauregard's
same idea expressed in backwoods idiom

Colonel Carroll: General, a heavy line of
infantry is in our rear. We're between two
lines of battle. What'll we do?

General Forrest: Charge both ways!

—Brice's Cross Roads

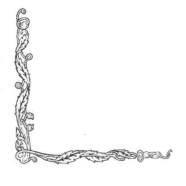
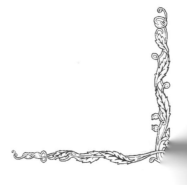

Never stand and take a charge. . . . charge
them too.

—*Nathan Bedford Forrest*

Whenever you meet the enemy, no matter how few there are of you or how many
of them, show fight.

—*Nathan Bedford Forrest*

I will often have
need of this maneuver,
as it will be necessary from
time to time for me to show
more men than I actually
have on the field.

*—Forrest to a Confederate drill instructor
referring to a bugle call that would order
his men to form a circle*

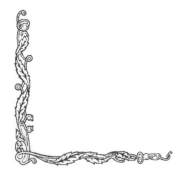
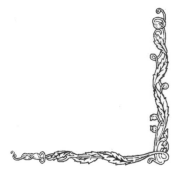

No device for creating this impression was too insignificant to be called into play. The constant beating of kettledrums, the lighting and tending of numerous fires, moving artillery pieces from one point to another, the dismounting of cavalry and parading them as infantry— nothing was overlooked.

—*Captain John Morton, describing the methods Forrest used to deceive the enemy and give the impression that he had more men and guns than he actually did*

When Streight saw they were barely four hundred, he did rear! demanded to have his arms back and that we should fight it out. I just laughed at him and patted him on the shoulder and said: "Ah, Colonel, all is fair in love and war you know."

—*Forrest, after bluffing Colonel Abel Streight into surrendering a force three times the size of his own, May 3, 1863*

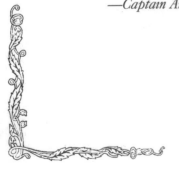

Cheer up, Colonel, this is not the first time a bluff has beat a straight.

—*Captain Anderson to Colonel Streight after his surrender to Forrest's smaller force*

Braxton Bragg

CHAPTER TWO

Vain Efforts and Stolen Victories

Too often, Forrest's hardest battles were fought against the entrenched, elements in his own army that were conservative to the point of ineptitude. They posed a greater threat to the survival of the Southern Confederacy than any marauding blue-coats. Forrest whipped the Yankees in every battle he fought as the general of record. Yet these victories were achieved despite the apparent indifference of a Confederate high command out of touch with the actual situation in the field. Time and again, troops Forrest had recruited, trained, equipped and baptized with fire were reassigned to other commands or detached for ill-advised, half-measure operations. Indeed, the scattered passive-defensive posture of the Confederate forces in the West, led by Richmond-sponsored generals more adept at political intrigue than winning battles, was more obstacle than boon to Forrest's success.

In his reports covering his activities, from his first action in Kentucky to his direction of Hood's evacuation from Tennessee, Forrest offered realistic assessments commending the performance of his men and devoid of self-praise. No general officer left a more impressive paper trail. Forrest is on record opposing the decisions of Wheeler at Dover, Bragg at Chickamauga, and Hood at Franklin. In each instance, subsequent events proved his judgment correct.

After President Jefferson Davis read the reports of Forrest's 1864 campaign across the Tennessee River, he was spurred to seek out and study

Forrest's earlier communications. By his own admission, Davis discovered Forrest's breadth of understanding of the overall strategic situation more than a decade later. In a conversation between Davis and Governor James D. Porter that took place during Forrest's funeral procession in Memphis, the former Confederate chief executive is reported to have lamented, "I saw it all after it was too late."

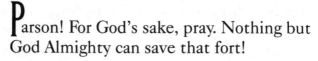

Parson! For God's sake, pray. Nothing but God Almighty can save that fort!

> —*Forrest to a chaplain at Fort Donelson,*
> *February 14, 1862*

I am clearly of the opinion that two-thirds of our army could have marched out without loss, and that, had we encountered the fight the next day, we should have gained a glorious victory.

> —*Nathan Bedford Forrest in his report on*
> *the Confederate surrender at*
> *Fort Donelson, 1862*

I did not come here for the purpose of surrendering my command.

> —*Nathan Bedford Forrest, Fort Donelson, 1862*

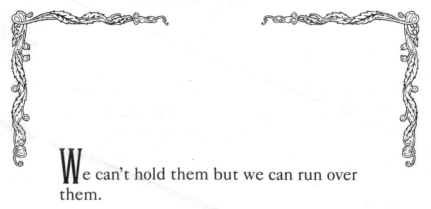

We can't hold them but we can run over them.

—Nathan Bedford Forrest to Gideon Pillow,
Fort Donelson

All right; I admire your loyalty, but damn your judgment!

—Forrest to a soldier who would not leave Fort Donelson
with Forrest's command, wishing to share
the fate of his comrades, 1862

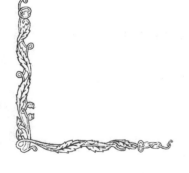

We'll be whipped like hell tomorrow.

*—General Forrest to General William J. Hardee on the
night of April 7, 1862— before the Union's
victorious counterattack at Shiloh*

I have protested against the move, but my protest has been disregarded and I intend to do my whole duty, and I want my men to do the same. . . . If I am killed in this fight, you will see that justice is done by officially stating that I protested against the attack, and that I am not willing to he held responsible for any disaster that may result.

*—Forrest to his aides on the attack at Dover,
near Fort Donelson, February 3, 1863*

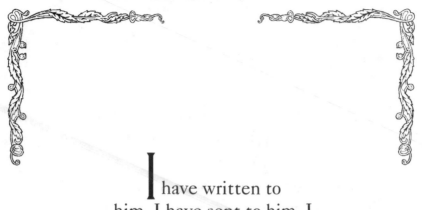

I have written to
him. I have sent to him. I
have given him information of
the condition of the Federal
army. What does he
fight battles for?

—Forrest on Braxton Bragg, when Bragg did not
follow up his victory at Chickamauga, 1863

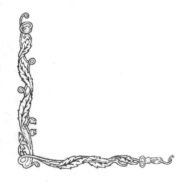
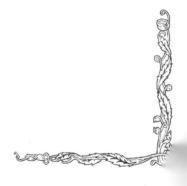

No, he'll never
say a word about it; he'll
be the last man to mention it;
and mark my word, he'll take no
action in the matter. I will ask to
be relieved and transferred to
a different field, and he
will not oppose it.

*—Forrest on Bragg, concerning the former's
tirade against the latter*

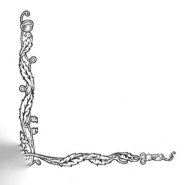
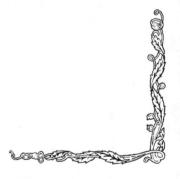

To my mind it is evident that the end is not far off; it will be a question of time as to when General Lee's lines at Petersburg will be broken, for Grant is wearing him out; with unlimited resources of men and money, he must ultimately force Lee to leave Virginia or surrender.

—*Nathan Bedford Forrest, early 1865*

Every moment lost is worth the life of a thousand men.

—*Nathan Bedford Forrest to Braxton Bragg,
Chickamauga, September 18-20, 1863*

If you ever again try to interfere with me or cross my path, it will be at the peril of your life.

—*Nathan Bedford Forrest to Braxton Bragg, 1863*

I will be in my coffin before I will fight again under your command.

—*Nathan Bedford Forrest to Major General Joseph Wheeler, Dover, 1863*

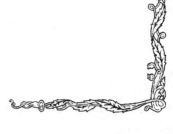

I do not think the Federals will stand strong pressure from the front; the show of force they are making is a feint in order to hold me back from a more vigorous pursuit.

—*General John Bell Hood, Franklin, 1864*

General Hood, if you will give me one strong division of infantry with my cavalry, I will agree to flank the Federals from their works within two hours' time.

—*Nathan Bedford Forrest, Franklin, 1864. Hood denied Forrest's request. Instead, he dashed the Army of Tennessee to pieces against the Union breastworks. One-fifth of the army was lost; five general officers were killed, six wounded, and one captured. Forrest biographer Andrew Lytle wrote, "In thirty-five days [Hood] had destroyed the Army of Tennessee."*

A. P. Hill

CHAPTER THREE

The Serious Business of Fighting

In many respects, Nathan Bedford Forrest could be described as having a micro-managerial leadership style. Such modern classifications from the business world are particularly apt when considering that Forrest came from a business background, dealing in cotton and human chattel. In Forrest's cavalry, there was a right way and a wrong way to do everything. Whether crossing a ditch or a river, tethering a horse, folding a saddle blanket, or sharpening a saber his men were prepared for every contingency through specific instructions and by Forrest's own example.

Micro-managers are correct in believing that their success hinges on attention to detail. However, their downfall often stems from an inability to discriminate between what is truly significant and what is trivial. Forrest never suffered from this misplaced preoccupation with the trivial. As a master of the march, battle, pursuit, and, when expedient, what Wyeth called "the science and art of running," he fought to inflict the maximum number of losses on the enemy. Even so, no detail was too small to contribute to this larger goal. The sabers his officers carried offer a literal case in point. Although the short Enfield or the Navy six-shooter was much preferred at close quarters, in worst-case scenarios, Forrest's men could count on razor-edged weapons. The sabers were honed sharp the entire length of the blade rather than only at the tip, as was the prevailing custom.

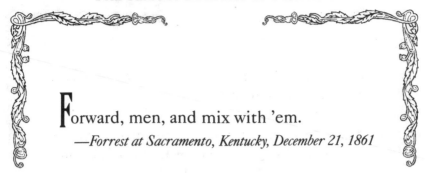

Forward, men, and mix with 'em.

—*Forrest at Sacramento, Kentucky, December 21, 1861*

Boys, do you hear that musketry and that artillery? It means that our friends are falling by the hundreds at the hands of the enemy, and we are here guarding a damned creek! Let's go and help them. What do you say?

—*Forrest to his men at Shiloh, 1862*

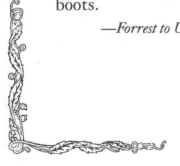

I've got enough to whip you out of your boots.

—*Forrest to Union Colonel Streight, May 3, 1863*

Colonel Forrest: I cannot permit my men to remain here under fire; I will have either to move forward or backward.

General Cheatham: I cannot give you orders; if you make the charge, it will be on your own responsibility.

Colonel Forrest: Then I'll do it.

—*Shiloh, 1862*

I did not come here to make a half job of it. I mean to have them all.

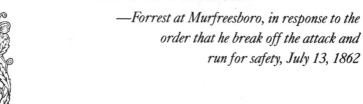

—*Forrest at Murfreesboro, in response to the order that he break off the attack and run for safety, July 13, 1862*

Get 'em scared, and then keep the scare of 'em.

—Nathan Bedford Forrest to his artillery commander John Watson Morton at Brice's Cross Roads, June 1864

General Forrest, I wish to congratulate you and those brave men moving across that field like veteran infantry upon their magnificent behavior.

—General D. H. Hill on Forrest's troops at Chickamauga

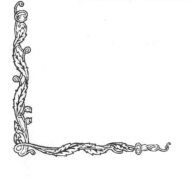

He shall not cook a meal or have a night's sleep, and I will wear his army to a frazzle before he gets out of the country.

> —*Forrest to General Stephen D. Lee concerning the pursuit of Union General Smith*

War means fighting, and fighting means killing.

> —*Nathan Bedford Forrest*

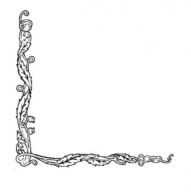

General Forrest: Where is the enemy's whole position?

Colonel Barteau: You see it, General, and they are preparing to charge.

General Forrest: Then we will charge them.

—*Okolona, Mississippi, 1864*

I saw Grierson make a "bad move" and then I rode right over him.

—*Nathan Bedford Forrest, Okolona, 1864. The term
bad move was one he associated with checkers,
a game Forrest never lost.*

Tell Bell to move up fast and fetch all he's got.

—*Forrest to Colonel Tyree H. Bell at Brice's Cross Roads*

When you hear his guns, and the bugle sounds, every man must charge, and we will give them hell.

—*Forrest to his men at Brice's Cross Roads*

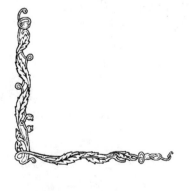

If that boy had known enough to give me the point of his saber instead of the edge, I should not have been here to tell you about it.

*—Forrest to General Wilson after the battle
of Selma, Alabama, April 2, 1865*

If you surrender, you shall be treated as prisoners of war, but if I have to storm your works, you may expect no quarter.

—Nathan Bedford Forrest

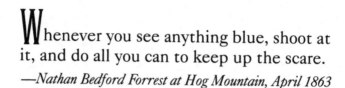

Whenever you see anything blue, shoot at it, and do all you can to keep up the scare.

—*Nathan Bedford Forrest at Hog Mountain, April 1863*

Captain Morton: I was afraid they might take my guns.

General Forrest: Well, artillery is made to be captured, and I wanted to see them take yours.

—*Brice's Cross Roads*

You may tell the general for me, that I am going back on the same road I came by, and if we meet, I promise to whip him out of his boots.

—*Forrest to an aide of Union General Washburn*

Does the damned fool want to be blown up? Well, I'll blow him up, then. Give him hell, Captain Morton—as hot as you've got it, too.

—*Forrest at Athens, Alabama, 1864*

There is no doubt we could soon wipe old Sherman off the face of the earth, John, if they'd give me enough men and you enough guns.

—*Forrest to Captain John Morton, 1864*

General Robert E. Lee

CHAPTER FOUR

Old Bedford

Perhaps no other Confederate chieftain, save Robert E. Lee, was more idolized by his men than Nathan Bedford Forrest. No doubt, victory inspired such cultlike adulation. Its bittersweet memory extended long beyond the duration of the war. In 1877, Forrest died at age fifty-six, wasted away by a chronic malady. Overwrought by emotion, thousands of gray-clad veterans turned out to escort the Old Man to his final resting place.

General Forrest had transformed these ordinary citizens—clerks, tailors, farmers, doctors, lawyers—into one of the finest fighting forces in

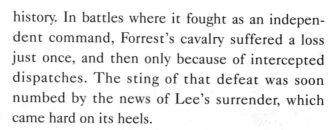

history. In battles where it fought as an independent command, Forrest's cavalry suffered a loss just once, and then only because of intercepted dispatches. The sting of that defeat was soon numbed by the news of Lee's surrender, which came hard on its heels.

Forrest lacked the inclination to expound upon, much less embellish, his own role in combat and instead credited the actions of his men. He loved them for their courage and loyalty but would not hesitate to shoot a soldier—usually a fleeing color-bearer—who had lost his wits in battle. (Braxton Bragg, in contrast, had a soldier court-martialed and shot for stealing apples.) For Forrest, cowards were catalysts of fear, who demoralized his unit and turned a retreat into a rout.

✲ ✲ ✲

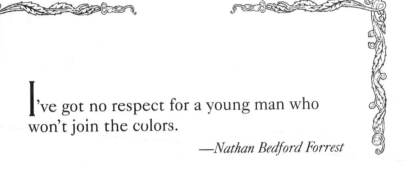

I've got no respect for a young man who won't join the colors.

—Nathan Bedford Forrest

I have no fault to find with my men. In both charges they did their duty as they have always done.

—General Forrest to General Joseph Wheeler
on the attack on Dover, 1863

I cannot speak in too high terms of the conduct of my whole command.

—Forrest on the conduct of his men at
Thompson's Station, March 5, 1863

Come on boys, if you want a heap of fun
and to kill some Yankees.

—Forrest's typical recruitment inducement

Men, do as I say and I will always lead you
to victory.

*—Nathan Bedford Forrest to his men before
the assault on Fort Pillow, April 1864*

Brave man; none braver!

*—Forrest on the death of Captain Freeman
at Franklin, April 10, 1863*

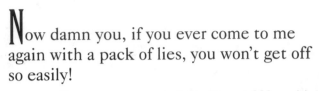

Now damn you, if you ever come to me
again with a pack of lies, you won't get off
so easily!

> *—Forrest to a courier who had been told by a citizen*
> *that a column of Yankees was nearby*

It's nothing but a damned little pistol ball!

> *—Forrest after being shot by one of his*
> *subordinates, June 1863*

General, I shall not be here long, and I was
not willing to go away without seeing you
in person and saying to you how thankful I
am that I am the one who is to die and that
you are spared to the country.

> *—Lieutenant A. W. Gould. Accused of cowardice by*
> *Forrest and transferred, Gould returned to*
> *murder Forrest and was himself*
> *mortally wounded.*

We had that confidence in him [Forrest] which I imagine the Old Guard had in Napoleon.

—*A lieutenant of Forrest's escort*

I will share the fate of my men.

—*Forrest to Major Anderson, 1865*

General Forrest was not cruel, nor necessarily severe, but he would not be trifled with.

—*Anonymous officer under Forrest's command*

Now, damn you, go back to the front and fight; you might as well be killed there as here, for if you ever run away again, you'll not get off so easy.

—Forrest to a trooper who was trying to run away from a fight at Ellis's Bridge near West Point, Mississippi, 1864

My God, men, will you see them kill your general? I will go to his rescue if not a man follows me!

—Colonel McCulloch to his men when Forrest was engaged in hand-to-hand fighting with Federal troops at Okolona, Mississippi

I'll officer you.

—Forrest, with saber drawn, to a young lieutenant who would not help in dousing flames on supply wagons set on fire by Union troops on their retreat to Memphis

Soldiers, the old campaign is ended, and your commanding general deems this an appropriate occasion to speak of the steadiness, self-denial, and patriotism with which you have borne the hardships of the last year.

—Forrest to his men after the campaign
with John Bell Hood

If your course has been marked by the graves of patriotic heroes who have fallen by your side, it has, at the same time, been more plainly marked by the blood of the invader.

—Forrest in early 1865

Preserve untarnished the reputation you have so nobly won.

—Part of Forrest's last address to his men, 1865

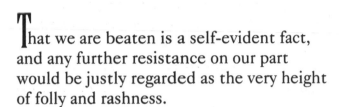

That we are beaten is a self-evident fact, and any further resistance on our part would be justly regarded as the very height of folly and rashness.

—Forrest to his men, 1865

Doctor, do all you can for those poor fellows.

*—Nathan Bedford Forrest speaking of the
wounded to Dr. J. B. Cowan*

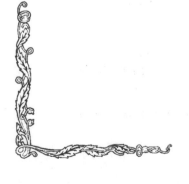

Major Anderson: Which way, General? General Forrest: Either. If one road led to hell and the other to Mexico, I would be indifferent as to which to take.

—Exchange before Forrest's decision to surrender his command

I have never on the field of battle sent you where I was unwilling to go myself, nor would I now advise you to a course which I felt myself unwilling to pursue. You have been good soldiers. You can be good citizens. Obey the laws, preserve your honor, and the government to which you have surrendered can afford to be and will be magnanimous.

—Nathan Bedford Forrest

Civil war, such as you
have just passed through,
naturally engenders feelings of
animosity, hatred and revenge. It is
our duty to divest ourselves of all such
feelings, and, so far as it is in our power
to do so, to cultivate feelings toward those
with whom we have so long contested, and
heretofore so widely but honestly dif-
fered. Whatever your responsibilities
may be to government, to society,
or to individuals, meet
them like men.

—*Nathan Bedford Forrest,*
farewell address to his men,
May 9, 1865

Joseph E. Johnston

CHAPTER FIVE

Contemporaries in Gray

Given the number of Confederate and Union troops engaged in the confrontations fought by Forrest's cavalry, a majority of actions did not require Old Bedford's careful coordination of all phases of the attack. Never in the rear, Forrest always placed himself in the thickest part of the fighting, astride one of the twenty-nine horses shot from under him during the course of the war.

Much has been written about Forrest's role as an innovator in the field of military science. Yet, in some respects, his methods were more a throwback to earlier times. Forrest's character in battle was typified by his

penchant for personal combat, reminiscent of Alexander the Great or some later Visigothic chieftain. Like any great commander, Forrest knew his presence on the frontlines ensured the best performance from his soldiers.

Each of the Confederate notables quoted in the following pages falls into one of two categories. Either he recognized Forrest's ability in his heyday, probably after witnessing his comportment under fire, as was the case with D. H. Hill and, early on, even an unbiased Bragg. Or he stuck by his prejudices until after the war, when history dictated the recognition the commander deserved. In fact, some of the postwar statements seem to be attempts to mask the prior assessments of their authors. Nonetheless, dispatches dating from the time clearly illustrate the earlier sentiments of some of Forrest's fellow officers; for example, when General Joseph E. Johnston did not take Forrest seriously late in 1863 when he was briefed on the raider's plans to hold West Tennessee.

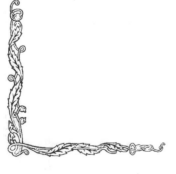

I doubt if any commander since the days of lion-hearted Richard killed as many enemies with his own hand as Forrest.

—General Richard Taylor on Forrest

I would ask for no better fortune if again placed on a flank, than to have such a vigilant, gallant and accomplished officer guarding its approaches.

—D. H. Hill in his official report at Chickamauga

General Forrest was born a soldier as men are born poets.

—*General Dabney H. Maury, who was himself a pioneer in the use of mounted infantry*

The man is ignorant, and does not know anything of cooperation. He is nothing but a good raider.

—*General Braxton Bragg on General N. B. Forrest*

Give Forrest a chance and he will distinguish himself.

—*Colonel Samuel Tate to General Albert Sydney Johnston in late October 1861*

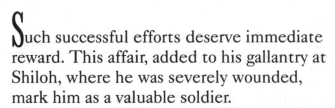

Such successful efforts deserve immediate reward. This affair, added to his gallantry at Shiloh, where he was severely wounded, mark him as a valuable soldier.

—*General Braxton Bragg to General Edmund Kirby Smith on Forrest's raid at Murfreesboro*

The truth may as well be told—he was unfit to serve under a superior; he was like a caged lion on the field of battle where he was not himself commanding.

—*David C. Kelley, longtime friend and staff officer of Forrest*

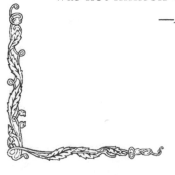

I would feel proud either in commanding or cooperating with so gallant an officer as yourself and one who has such an established reputation in the cavalry service to which I have been recently assigned.

—*General Stephen D. Lee to Forrest, on Forrest's transfer to his command*

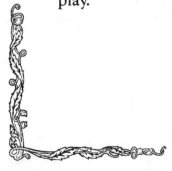

Forrest's capacity of war seemed only to be limited by the opportunities for its display.

—*General P. G. T. Beauregard*

One of his many peculiarities was that in battle he never seemed to touch the saddle, but "stood up" in his stirrups, an attitude which gave him the appearance of being a foot taller than he really was. As he was over six feet in stature and large proportions and of necessity rode a large horse, it was not difficult to recognize his imposing presence at an ordinary distance along the line.

—*Description of Forrest by Colonel C. R. Barteau*

Forrest, who, had he the advantages of a thoroughly military education and training, would have been the great central figure of the Civil War.

—*General Joseph E. Johnston after the war*

General P. G. T. Beauregard

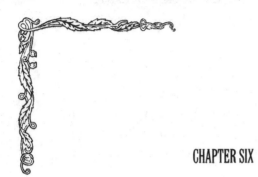

CHAPTER SIX

Contemporaries in Blue

Largely ignored or underutilized by the Rebel armies to which his irregulars were attached, Forrest's activities and operations were commonly the result of his own initiative and imagination. Left to his own devices, he never failed to strike the Federal army where it hurt most. Forrest got the enemy's attention by interrupting communication and supply lines, tearing up railroads, and overwhelming undermanned outposts.

The frequent appearance of Forrest's name in

Union communications bears little relation to the actual size or authority of his command. The Union's preoccupation with Forrest, as detailed in its dispatches, is perhaps the most convincing testament to his effectiveness as a soldier.

I regret very much that I could not have the pleasure of bringing you his hair, but he is too great a plunderer to fight anything like an equal force.

—*General Samuel D. Sturgis to*
General William T. Sherman

For God's sake, if Mr. Forrest will let me alone, I will let him alone.

—*General Samuel D. Sturgis*

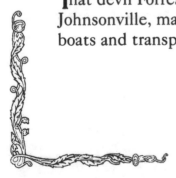

That devil Forrest was down about Johnsonville, making havoc among the gunboats and transports.

—*General William T. Sherman to*
General Ulysses S. Grant, 1864

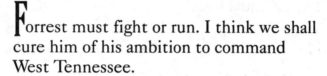

Forrest must fight or run. I think we shall cure him of his ambition to command West Tennessee.

—*General Stephen A. Hurlbut, 1863*

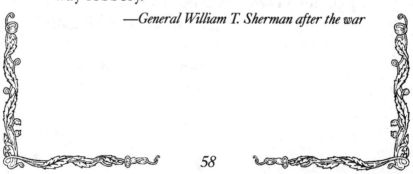

Such men as Wade Hampton, Forrest, Wirt Adams, et cetera, never will work and nothing is left for them but death or highway robbery.

—*General William T. Sherman after the war*

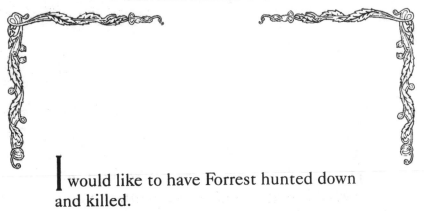

I would like to have Forrest hunted down and killed.

—*General William T. Sherman to General George H. Thomas, January 1864*

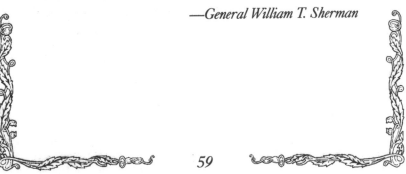

Follow Forrest to the death if it costs 10,000 lives and breaks the Treasury. There will never be peace in Tennessee till Forrest is dead.

—*General William T. Sherman*

After all, I think Forrest was the most remarkable man our Civil War produced on either side.

—*William T. Sherman after the war*

Writing words, General Forrest was governed by sound, and his spelling, like his fighting, was the shortest way to the end.

—*Major Charles Anderson*

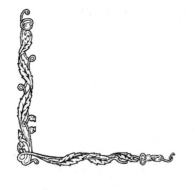
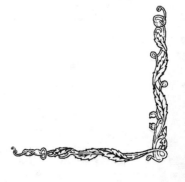

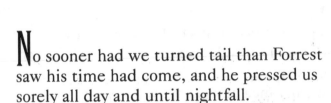

No sooner had we turned tail than Forrest saw his time had come, and he pressed us sorely all day and until nightfall.

—*Colonel Waring of General Smith's command at Ellis's Bridge, February 21, 1864*

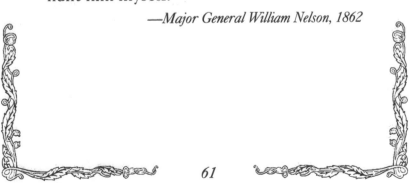

I will have about twelve hundred cavalry, and Mr. Forrest shall have no rest. I will hunt him myself.

—*Major General William Nelson, 1862*

He seemed always to know what I was doing or intended to do, while I am free to confess I could never tell or form any satisfactory idea of what he was trying to accomplish.

—*William T. Sherman after the war*

Send all your cavalry with orders to find him and destroy him wherever found.

—*General Ulysses S. Grant to William T. Sherman after Forrest's repulse at Paducah, Kentucky*

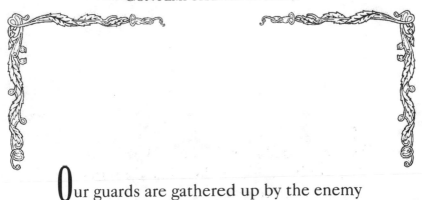

Our guards are gathered up by the enemy as easily as he would herd cattle.

—*General Don Carlos Buell, 1862*

The rear guard, however, was undaunted and firm, and did its work bravely to the last.

—*General George H. Thomas speaking of Forrest's protection of Hood's Army of Tennessee on its retreat from Nashville*

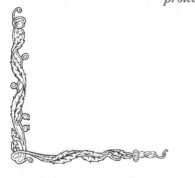

General John Bell Hood

CHAPTER SEVEN

The Unknown Devil

If Robert E. Lee embodies the last and fullest flowering of the Southern gentry, Nathan Bedford Forrest represents the sheer will of the self-made frontiersman. Uneducated but not illiterate, as is supposed (though his facility with English barely rose above the idiomatic), Forrest excelled at every vocation he genuinely pursued. The war destroyed his fortune, but in the postbellum period, he was able to repair his finances to some extent before his body gave out. In addition to providing for his own family and dependents, Forrest fulfilled the many promises he had made to dying soldiers, and guaranteed that their widows and children were not in need.

Nonetheless, sensational accounts of wartime atrocities dogged Forrest's name, and he was anathematized in the Northern press. During Reconstruction, he was suspected of being a ringleader in the network of Neo-Confederate secret societies that were active, especially in Tennessee. These accusations tainted Forrest's image and his activities were never fully known. His role remains enigmatic.

Ultimately eschewing violence for peace, Forrest's last years bear witness to the deep compassion, tenderness, and even humor he had exhibited at moments throughout his hard life. In a deathbed interview with John T. Morgan, he admitted: "General, I am broken in health and spirit, and have not long to live. My life has been a battle from the start. It was a fight to achieve a livelihood for those dependent upon me in my younger days, and an independence for myself when I grew up to manhood, as well as in the terrible turmoil

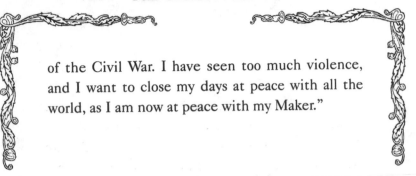

of the Civil War. I have seen too much violence, and I want to close my days at peace with all the world, as I am now at peace with my Maker."

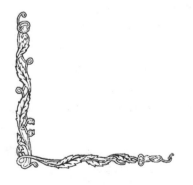
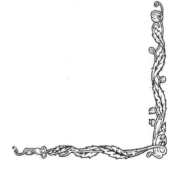

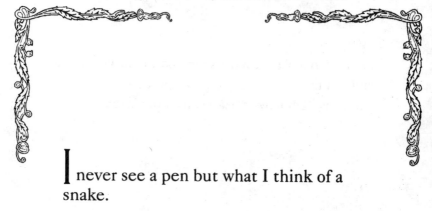

I never see a pen but what I think of a snake.

—*Nathan Bedford Forrest*

I am also aware that I am at this moment regarded in large communities, in the North, with great abhorrence, as a detestable monster, ruthless and swift to take life.

—*Nathan Bedford Forrest*

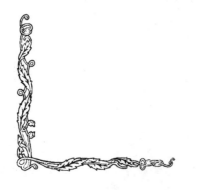

No one knows the embarrassment I labor under when thrown in the company of educated persons.

—*Nathan Bedford Forrest*

No; I'll be damned if I can.

—*Forrest in response to a friend who asked*
if he could not control his temper

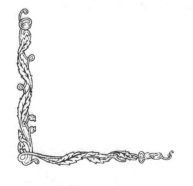

My staff does all my drinking.

—*Nathan Bedford Forrest*

What I desire most of you, my son, is never to gamble or swear. These are baneful vices.

—*Forrest in a letter to his son, William,*
dated April 15, 1865

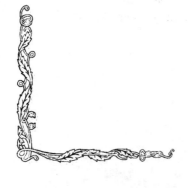

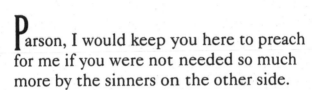

Parson, I would keep you here to preach for me if you were not needed so much more by the sinners on the other side.

> —*Forrest to a captured chaplain of the Union army*

There is no time to saddle a horse; get up here behind me. Don't be uneasy; I will bring her back safe.

> —*Forrest to a young girl and her mother. The girl gave information to Forrest's rebels about where to ford a creek to escape pursuing Yankees.*

Any man who is in favor of a further prosecution of this war is a fit subject for a lunatic asylum, and ought to be sent there immediately.

—*Nathan Bedford Forrest*

Men, you may all do as you damn please, but I'm a-goin' home.

—*Forrest to Charles Clark, governor of Mississippi and Isham G. Harris, former governor of Tennessee, in response to the request that he keep fighting*

I did all in my
power to break up the
government, but I have found
it a useless undertaking, and am
now resolved to stand by the
government as earnestly and
as honestly as I fought.

—*Nathan Bedford Forrest,*
after the war

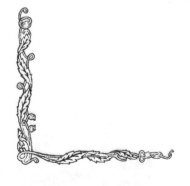

My strength is failing and it is absolutely necessary that I should have some rest.

—*Forrest to General Richard Taylor, late 1864*

I went into the army worth a million and a half dollars, and came out a beggar.

—*Nathan Bedford Forrest*

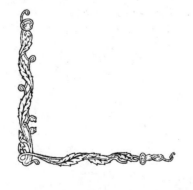

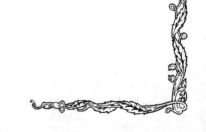

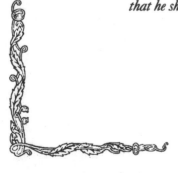

I came out of the war pretty well wrecked . . . completely used up. shot all to pieces, crippled up . . . a beggar.

—*Nathan Bedford Forrest*

This is my country. I am hard at work upon my plantation, and carefully observing the obligations of my parole. If the Federal government does not regard it they will be sorry. I shall not go away.

—*Nathan Bedford Forrest, in response to a suggestion that he should leave the country to avoid being arrested and tried for treason*

The whole of West Tennessee is overrun by bands and squads of robbers, horse thieves and deserters, whose depredations and unlawful appropriations of private property are rapidly depleting the country.

—*Nathan Bedford Forrest, March 1864*

We were born on the same soil, breathe the same air, live on the same land, and why should we not be brothers and sisters?

—*Nathan Bedford Forrest, addressing the African-American community of Memphis at the city fairgrounds, July 5, 1875*

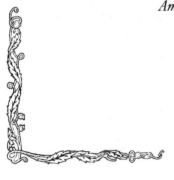

We have already
lost all but honor by
the last war, and I must say,
that in order to be men, we must
protect our honor at all hazards
and we must also protect our
homes and families.

—Nathan Bedford Forrest

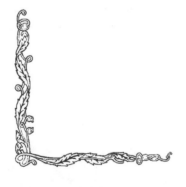

I want our country quiet once more, and I want to see our people united and working together harmoniously.

—*Nathan Bedford Forrest*

I stand by the government as earnestly and honestly as I fought it.

—*Nathan Bedford Forrest*

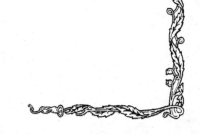

It is only necessary to turn to the official documents of Tennessee to show that all Forrest said about the alarm which prevailed during the administration of Governor Brownlow was strictly true. No state was ever reduced to such humiliation and degradation as that unhappy commonwealth during the years Brownlow ruled over her.

—Report of the House Congressional Committee that interviewed Forrest in 1871-72 regarding the Ku Klux Klan

Abolish the Loyal League and the Ku Klux Klan; let us come together and stand together.

—Nathan Bedford Forrest, calling for an end to civil unrest

Call my wife.

*—Last coherent words of
General Nathan Bedford Forrest*

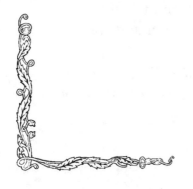
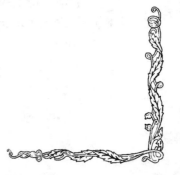

ISBN 1-888952-35-0

6 10529 00047 6